Rememberings of an Adventurer

If you find this travel journal I am probably lost somewhere, trying to get directions from a goatherder or burning the last of my postcards for warmth in the cold, cold night.
So, by returning this book, you would not only make me very happy, but could also make my life much warmer. Thanks. You're great.

Name:

Mobile:

Email:

Officialness and important facts about me

Passport details:

Driving licence:

Travel insurance:

Emergency contact number:

Blood group:

Medical weirdness (allergies, conditions, third nipples etc.):

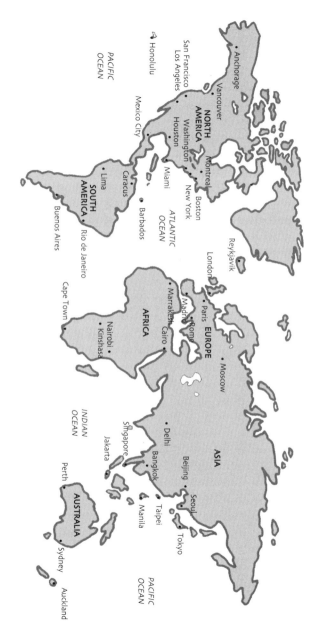

Country Information

Country	Capital	Currency	Code	GMT
Australia	Canberra	Australian Dollar	61	+8/10
Austria	Vienna	Euro	43	+1
Belgium	Brussels	Euro	32	+1
Brazil	Brasilia	Real	55	-3
Canada	Ottawa	Canadian Dollar	1	-4/8
Chile	Santiago	Peso	56	-4
China	Beijing	Yuan	86	+8
Denmark	Copenhagen	Danish Krone	45	+1
Egypt	Cairo	Egyptian Pound	20	+2
Finland	Helsinki	Euro	358	+2
France	Paris	Euro	33	+1
Germany	Berlin	Euro	49	+1
Greece	Athens	Euro	30	+2
Guatemala	Guatemala City	Quetzal	502	-6
Hong Kong	-	Hong Kong Dollar	852	+8
India	New Delhi	Indian Rupee	91	+5 1/2
Ireland	Dublin	Euro	353	0
Italy	Rome	Euro	39	+1
Jamaica	Kingston	Jamaican Dollar	1809	-5
Japan	Tokyo	Yen	81	+9
Kenya	Nairobi	Kenyan Shilling	254	+3

Country Information

Country	Capital	Currency	Code	GMT
Mexico	Mexico City	Peso	52	-6
Morocco	Rabat	Dirham	212	0
Nepal	Kathmandu	Nepalese Rupee	977	+5 3/4
Netherlands	Amsterdam	Euro	31	+1
New Zealand	Wellington	NZ Dollar	64	+12
Norway	Oslo	Norwegian Krone	47	+1
Peru	Lima	Sol	51	-5
Portugal	Lisbon	Euro	351	0
Puerto Rico	San Juan	US Dollar	1787	-4
Russia	Moscow	Rouble	7	+2 1/2
Singapore	-	Singapore Dollar	65	+8
South Africa	Pretoria	Rand	27	+2
Spain	Madrid	Euro	34	+1
Sri Lanka	Colombo	Sri Lankan Rupee	94	+5 1/2
Sweden	Stockholm	Swedish Krona	46	+1
Switzerland	Bern	Swiss Franc	41	+1
Thailand	Bangkok	Baht	66	+7
Tunisia	Tunis	Tunisian Dinar	216	+1
Turkey	Ankara	Turkish Lira	91	+2
UK	London	Pound	44	0
USA	Washington DC	US Dollar	1	-5/9

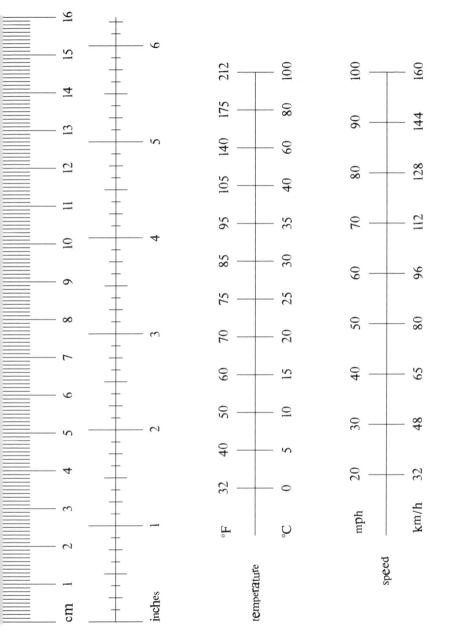

Conversion Charts

Ounces		Grams
0.035	1	28.3
0.176	5	141
0.35	10	283

Pounds		Kilograms
2.20	1	0.45
11.02	5	2.27
22.05	10	4.54
110.23	50	22.68
220.46	100	45.36

Pints		Litres
1.76	1	0.57
8.8	5	2.84
17.6	10	5.68

Inches		Centimetres
0.394	1	2.54
1.97	5	12.7
3.94	10	25.4
19.7	50	127

Feet		Metres
3.28	1	0.30
16.4	5	1.52
32.81	10	3.04
164	50	15.2
328	100	30.4

Miles		Kilometres
0.62	1	1.61
6.21	10	16.09
31.07	50	80.46
62.14	100	160.93

Clothing Sizes

Men's
Suits and coats

British	36	38	40	42	44	46	48
American	36	38	40	42	44	46	48
Continental	46	48	50	52	54	56	58

Shirts

British	14	14.5	15	15.5	16	16.5	17	17.5
American	14	14.5	15	15.5	16	16.5	17	17.5
Continental	36	37	38	39	41	42	43	44

Women's
Dresses and suits

British	6	8	10	12	14	16	18	20
American	4	6	8	10	12	14	16	18
Continental	34	36	38	40	42	44	46	50

Men's Shoes

British	6	7	8	9	10	11	12	13
American	6.5	7.5	8.5	9.5	10.5	11.5	12.5	13.5
Continental	38.5	40	42	43.5	44.5	45.5	46.5	47.5

Women's Shoes

British	3	4	5	6	7	8	9.5
American	5.5	6.5	7.5	8.5	9.5	10.5	12
Continental	35.5	37	38	39	41	43	44

Other useful info

Useful phrases

English	French	German	Italian	Spanish
hello	bonjour	guten tag	ciao	hola
goodbye	au revoir	auf wiedersehen	arrivederci	adiós
please	s'il vous plaît	bitte	per favore	por favor
thank you	merci	danke	grazie	gracias
how much?	combien?	wie viel?	quanto?	cuánto?
yes	oui	ja	si	sí
no	non	nein	no	no
I don't understand	je ne comprends pas	ich verstehe nicht	non capisco	no entiendo
toilet	toilette	toilette	gabinetto	tocado
sorry	pardon	entschuldigung	scusi	lo siento
Sir	Monsieur	Herr	Signore	Señor
Madam	Madame	Frau	Signora	Señora
I'm lost	Je suis perdu	Ich bin verloren	Sono perso	Estoy perdid
where is...	où se trouve...	wo ist...	dove si trova...	dónde está...
doctor	médecin	Arzt	medico	médico
police	police	Polizei	polizia	policía...
one	un	eins	uno	uno
two	deux	zwei	due	dos
three	trois	drei	tre	tres
four	quatre	vier	quattro	cuatro
five	cinq	funf	cinque	cinco
six	six	sechs	sei	seis
seven	sept	sieben	sette	siete
eight	huit	acht	otto	ocho
nine	neuf	neun	nove	nueve
ten	dix	zehn	dieci	diez

WanderLUSTrous

Notes about this oh-my-goodness-I'm-so-excited-I-might-pass-out trip I'm taking

paNT-
foldingly
prePAred
foR ANYthing

List of to-do-ness which I must absolutely complete before I go

Jabs what I've had

What	When	Never again?

Packing List-athon

Stuff I must absolutely remember to pack

Stuff I really do not need to bring, but probably will

Super important checklist of stuff that if I forget I will be in no small amount of trouble

Passport

Visas

Vaccination certificates

Travellers cheques

Credit/cash cards

Driving licence

Money belt

Two wallets

Alarm clock/watch

Camera

Camera batteries

Memory cards

Torch

Swiss army knife*

Travel guide

Phrase book

Travel clothes wash

Padlock

Matches/lighter

Playing cards

Pen/pencil

Water bottle

Gaffa tape

Sleeping sheet

Safety pins*

Mini sewing kit*

Ear plugs

Book

Pac-a-mac

Wet wipes

Tissues/toilet roll

Sun hat

Flip flops

Sunscreen

Lip balm

Fleece

Tiger balm

MP3 player

Band aids

Nail file*

Insect repellant

Towel

Diarrhoea tablets

*not in hand luggage

ItinEraRY

TAStiC

Itinerary Listings

Destination:

Departure details

Date:

From:

At: GMT

Flight number:

Arrival details

At: local time

Hand luggage checklist:

Other Connections

Destination:

Depart from:

At:

Flight no:

Arrive at:

Destination:

Depart from:

At:

Flight no:

Arrive at:

Destination:

Depart from:

At:

Flight no:

Arrive at:

Destination:

Depart from:

At:

Flight no:

Arrive at:

Destination:

Depart from:

At:

Flight no:

Arrive at:

Destination:

Depart from:

At:

Flight no:

Arrive at:

Destination:

Depart from:

At:

Flight no:

Arrive at:

Destination:

Depart from:

At:

Flight no:

Arrive at:

Accommodations I will be staying in

1 Name:

Address:

Contact tel:

Website:

Price: No. of nights:

Check in time: Check out time:

Other details:

2

Name:

Address:

Contact tel:

Website:

Price: No. of nights:

Check in time: Check out time:

Other details:

3

Name:

Address:

Contact tel:

Website:

Price: No. of nights:

Check in time: Check out time:

Other details:

Touristastic things I must see

Museums

Galleries

Churches and cathedrals and stuff

Mountains, lakes and green stuff

Beaches

Shops and markets

Off-the-beaten-trackness I must discover and ideas for adventurement

So Excited I Might Pop

Gameage & Things to Pass the Time

More TrAVeL ScriBblings By Me

ReMemBerings & ReminiscinGs NOtes from my Travels

Bestest things about my trip

Worstest things about my trip

I-almost-came-a-cropper-but-thankfully-didn't incidents

Stories which will keep me in dinner parties for years

tiny things I noticed

Really HUGE things which were un-not-noticeable

Animals and other furry, hairy and feathered stuff I have encountered

Things which have bitten / stung or Otherwise hurt me

A drawing / some notes about a historic building which looked a bit like the other 276 historic buildings I have seen

People happenings, funny conversations and stuff

Food which I put in my tummy like
soup made out of donkey hair

What I liked   What didn't like me

Drinks which drunk me

Moments of clarity and inspired ideas
(my god I'm a genius)

Random events which occurred

Spending diary

What I bought	When / Where	How much

What I bought	When / Where	How much

Lucky people who will get a postcard from me and feel jealous. HA!

Name	Address	Sent

Name	Address	Sent

Locally made crafts like a hat in the shape of a traditional sausage and other novelty items which I will buy for people and they will be grateful

What gift	For who	How much

What gift	For who	How much

Lovely people I met on my travels who I will most definitely keep in touch with / avoid

Name	Contact	Avoid

Name	Contact	Avoid?

Recommendations I must remember and pass on for this place I have been

Useful websites

I must go
and fiNd
MyseLf

OH here
I am

Things I am newly inspired to do when I get home

Other trips I'd love to take

Top travel tips what I have learnt the hard way

PAIYting thoughts